Clueless™

Cher's Guide to . . . Whatever

Cher *so* cares about making a difference, about making the world a happier and more beautiful place. Sometimes this means matchmaking, whether among the hotties or the style-impaired. Sometimes this means sharing her health and beauty secrets with ensembly challenged persons.

●

She's going to share her experience with you on such vital issues as why you should avoid dating high school boys, how to prepare for your road test, putting together a wardrobe that works for under six figures, the importance of accessories and attitude, and so much more.

Clueless™
•
Cher's Guide
to...
Whatever

H. B. GILMOUR

Based on the characters created by

AMY HECKERLING

AN ARCHWAY PAPERBACK
Published by POCKET BOOKS
New York   London   Toronto   Sydney   Tokyo   Singapore

AN ARCHWAY PAPERBACK *Original*

 An Archway Paperback published by
POCKET BOOKS, a division of
Simon & Schuster Inc.
1230 Avenue of the Americas, New York, NY 10020

™ and copyright © 1995 by Paramount Pictures

ISBN: 0-671-56865-5

First Archway Paperback printing September 1995

10   9   8

AN ARCHWAY PAPERBACK and colophon are registered trademarks of Simon & Schuster Inc.

Printed in the U.S.A.

IL 7+

Contents

Clueless™

·

Cher's Guide
to...
Whatever

Introduction

I am not the same Cher Horowitz I once was. And it's not just because my Baldwin of a boyfriend, Josh, taught me the importance of making a contribution to society. I mean, it's not like I never tried to help anyone before. *Au contraire.* My life has been practically dedicated to improvement. My own as much as everybody else's.

I am constantly refereeing my best friend Dionne's ultradramatic relationship with her rap-song-writing boyfriend, Murray. I transformed Tai, the new girl at school, from a Docs-wearing New York nihilist to a fabulously well-groomed Beverly Hills hottie. I sparked a total romance between two adorable teachers, Mr. Hall and Miss Geist. Some people suggested it was to get better grades.

Not even!

I have always had a furious interest in sharing my special gift.

Everyone has a gift. Everyone has a talent. Mine is makeovers.

I cannot even pass a drooping flower without wanting to water it—or at least asking José, our gardener, to do it.

I have a passion for perfection. In others as well as myself. My early years were spent furiously improving those I love.

Daddy, who is a fully prominent and ruthless attorney, rampantly relies on my reminders for his fashion and fitness needs.

I have purchased adorable designer uniforms for our overweight maid, Lucy, who would otherwise dust our classic *casa* in spandex tights and gem-studded T-shirts.

Josh, my ex-stepbrother and boyfriend (We are not blood relatives. Hello, this is not Kentucky. He just happens to be my father's third wife's son by her second marriage, okay?) . . . even Josh, who was always all serious and flanneled out, credits me with bringing out his lighter side. He laughs more now and reads paperbacks.

I have always cared about making a difference, about making the world a happier and more beautiful place. Sometimes this means matchmaking, whether among the hotties or the style-impaired. I am a monster matchmaker. The total best. Sometimes this means sharing my health and beauty secrets with ensembly challenged persons like Amber Salk.

I have always had a rampant interest in helping others. I've been doing makeovers practically since I was born.

So what has changed?

Experience. Experience is what has made the difference. I know so much more than I used to about life, love, and negotiating grades—and I'm here to help you!

I'm going to share my experience with you on such vital issues as why you should avoid dating high school boys, how to prepare for your road test, putting together a wardrobe that works for under six figures, the importance of accessories and attitude, and so much more.

Now you can avoid the pitfalls that push most high school students to the postal edge.

You can do it.

You can be a winner.

You can negotiate, manipulate, manage, and make over your academic and social life *totally*—with the help of this excellent, easy-to-follow guide to . . . whatever.

Accessories

A BETTY'S
BEST FRIEND

My best friend, Dionne, is one of *the* major Bettys of Beverly Hills. We're named for famous singers of our parents' generation who now do infomercials. De and I share a rampant interest in fashion. We believe that accessories are a vital aspect of the ensemble scene.

This just in from Webster, the dictionary man: An accessory is an article of dress, like gloves, that completes or enhances one's basic outfit.

I am not all *that* about gloves, but practically everyone I know is majorly into outfit enhancing. From backward caps and beepers to backpacks and nose rings, accessories can make or break a look.

Although everyone assures me I'm a genuine babe, I wouldn't say I'm brutally gorgeous, but I *so* know how to accessorize. So take my advice on this one.

Navel piercing and tattoos—get over it!

Skin is important. Without it, you'd just like leak all over. So what's up with poking holes in it?

Think of the future.

How's it going to look sitting around the pool at the retirement condo with like totally stretched-out holes in your belly and a wrinkled old eagle peeking out of your sleeve?

And tattoos? Please.

Just what I want for my birthday, a burnt-out biker artist putting holes in my skin and filling them with ink.

As if!

I'm really going to turn myself into a walking graffiti wall.

•

If you've got to body decorate, go faux!

It's important to have a sense of humor about accessories—and be willing to defend your choices.

De enjoys wearing tall top hats with her whimsical outfits. "Dude!" she greeted me one morning, climbing into the loqued-out Jeep Daddy bought me for my road test.

"Girlfriend!" I cried, peering over my shades at her hat. "Have you been shopping with Dr. Seuss?"

She eyed my faux fur bag. "At least I wouldn't skin my collie to make a back-pack," she said.

Tscha!

Attitude...

AND WHERE
TO GET IT

Attitude is the way you carry yourself,
the vibe you give off, your like essence or flavor.
To successfully make your presence
known in high school, you must have attitude.

People tell me that my attitude is seriously
self-assured but not reekingly so. De has a
soupçon of feisty peppering her confident
flair. Our friend Tai, who came from New
York City and looked it until De and I did
this monster makeover on her, has like
major Tootsie Pop attitude: tough on the
outside, but furiously sweet and soft within.
It's like she wears a sign that says, "Yo, don't
mess wit me . . . pretty please."

Everyone has attitude.
Everyone needs attitude. But
not everyone has the attitude
they need.

Slacker Attitude

Slumped shoulders, skateboards with decals all over them, wispy chin hair, thin dark socks that pool around your ankles, and trying to snag last night's homework from a passing valedictorian in the Quad is an attitude that screams Slacker.

This is not a very successful essence. And it is *so* last semester. Travis Birkenstock, Tai's admirer, used to reek Slacker attitude. But recently he joined a twelve-step program and is apologizing to practically everyone he meets on his new spiritual path.

High school is a major attitude-fest.

If you don't have an attitude, get one before the semester starts. It's required, not elective.

Here are some attitudes you may want to consider—and the places you can go to study them:

Perky, eager to please: The Body Shop.

Faux perky: McDonald's.

Perky, deeply self-assured: Cosmetics counters at Neiman Marcus, Saks, Bloomies, Burdines.

Perky, with it: Hairdressers under thirty.

Not perky, unimpressed, bored: Planet Hollywood, Hard Rock Café.

Serene, centered, superior: Yoga centers.

Perky, self-centered, superior: Frozen yogurt centers.

Blowing Off PE

AND OTHER FURIOUSLY BORING CLASSES

It's amazing how many brutally trivial subjects like physical education are offered in most high schools. And not just *offered*, but like forced upon you in the name of education. Please. Is there anyone out there who doesn't own her own videotape of *Cindy Crawford's Aerobicize* or *Buns of Steel*—or can't check it out of the library?

And it isn't like you really work out in PE. Physical education at my school is a sham. I mean, most of the time you're changing your clothes or waiting around for someone to reload the tennis-ball machine. Standing in line for forty minutes barely works off the calories in a stick of CareFree gum.

So here are some tested methods for bailing out of classes that offer little but employment for lonely adults who earn minor wages at a thankless job.

Schedule your cosmetic surgery strategically.

Between prep time and recuperation, you can avoid months of sports activity.

Creative preplanning works.

Take the time to come up with ten fully plausible excuses for getting out of class before you need them.

List these on individual index cards.

Discard after use.

Do not recycle excuses.
Teachers talk to each other.

Some examples:

Death of a family pet.

Cramps.

Boyfriend dumped you.

Prozac ran out.

Grandparent broke hip—
never use this more than four times in any
one semester.

Clothes

HOW TO MANAGE YOUR WARDROBE EVEN IF YOU DON'T HAVE THE PROPER SOFTWARE

Okay, so not everyone has every item of clothing they own loaded onto a PC software program.

Not everyone organizes her closet by color—left to right, white to cream on through the rainbow to black—broken into ensembles appropriate to activity and time of day . . . that's like school clothes to nighties, workout gear to evening wear.

But I do. It's like the only way I can even get dressed.

Not everyone's closet has racks that revolve just like at the French cleaners. Or a completely separate wall unit for shoes. Or accessories stacked in see-through Lucite containers.

Excuse me for needing neatness in my life. Some people are comfortable with chaos. I am totally not one of them.

And I also know that not everyone has charge cards to thirteen nationally franchised upscale stores or lives within two miles of three major malls.

But I do. It's furiously essential. If you were me you would definitely understand.

Clothing is more than a necessity for me, it's a passion.

Calvin Klein, Yves St. Laurent, Azzedine Alaïa—they're not just brand names to me, they're garment gurus.

Plus my school is ultracompetitive.

Dressing is practically an intramural event.

Shopping is the Olympics.

But the great thing about my being an expert in this area is that I can share my knowledge with you. With just a few tips, you can learn how to manage your wardrobe . . . even if you don't have the proper software!

Get your colors done.

If you're a spring-season kind of girl, be sure you fill your closets with loads of creamy pastels and subdued tones—unless there's a sale on an irresistible screaming electric blue or raging red number.

Then you go, girl.

It's hard to be an individualist in a world of ready-to-wear.

If you are a fashion trendsetter, you are going to have followers. Get used to it. Take it as a compliment. It's flattering. Be gracious.

Unless, of course, the person who is cloning you happens to be furiously self-centered and so full of herself she doesn't even get it that she's a rampant Monet—you know, like looks okay at a distance but is a total mess up close, not a babe, really.

A person, for instance, like Amber, who has fifty credit cards, no taste, a team of cosmetic surgeons on retainer, and a terminally negative attitude.

Tai and I went to this party in the Valley. We were just doing a lap before committing to a location when suddenly Tai tugged at the jacket sleeve of my amazing Alaïa micro-mini with its festive ruffle of black faux feathers.

"Hey," Tai said, pointing, "ain't that Amber in the same dress as yours?"

What a clone, I thought. "Excuse me," I said as Amber brushed by, "was that *you* going through my laundry?"

"As if!" she scoffed. "Like I would wear something from Judy's."

"I'd call you a fashion victim," I said, smiling politely, "but I understand you people prefer *ensembly challenged.*"

Never date a guy who dresses better than you. I mean, what would you bring to the relationship?

Daddy hated my friend Christian on first sight. Partly it was the way Christian dressed. The first time he came to our house he was styling in a vintage two-tone gabardine jacket from the fifties with a Frank Sinatra hat pushed back on his head.

"What's your story, kid?" Daddy growled, looking him over. "You think the death of Sammy Davis left an opening in the Rat Pack?" Then he added, "You drink?"

Christian said, "No, thanks, I'm cool."

"I'm not offering, idiot!" Daddy lost it. "I'm asking *if* you drink. What do you think, I give alcohol to teenage drivers taking my daughter out? No drinking and driving. If anything happens to Cher, I've got a forty-five and a shovel. I doubt anyone would miss you."

"Hey, man," Christian said, "the protective vibe. I can dig it."

Dating

THE DIFFERENCE BETWEEN HIGH SCHOOL BOYS AND REAL MEN

Is there something I'm supposed to say here? Like something the thirty-five major teen mags have missed and you don't already know?

As if!

High school is a vast wasteland when it comes to meeting mature quality guys. For me, that is. I'm only trying to share my personal experience.

In our school the best guys, the only ones to even consider dating, are in the clique called the Crew. De's boyfriend, Murray, is one of them. He wears huge baggy Calvins and a do-rag on his head. He's like very *GQ*, into the foremost urban togs major plastic can purchase. Murray drives a BMW and writes rap songs about career choices, investments, foreign-car maintenance, and other problems he's facing.

Tai also goes out with a high school guy, Travis. (See Slacker Attitude, page 11, and Spotting Slackers, page 26.)

I would never disrespect my friends' choices or deny their right to choose. But here are my deeply candid views on the subject:

High school boys are so high maintenance.

Like dogs. You have to walk them, feed them, practically give them flea baths, just so you can have some nervous creature jump and slobber all over you. Unfortunately, high school boys are the only guys you meet in high school.

It's better to wait than to lower your standards.

I don't mean to sound like a raging feminist, but when I think of all the time we spend on exercising, doing our hair, shopping, and makeup . . . whereas guys fall out of bed, put on a backward cap, and expect us to swoon. I guess I'm a traitor to my generation, but the way guys look now does nothing for me.

Picky is good when it comes to boys.

I believe in holding out for that really special someone. I mean, I'm like totally picky about my shoes, and they only go on my feet.

Spotting Slackers.

They're baked-out boneheads with Day-Glo decals on their skateboards. They wear knee-length cutoffs and tent-size T-shirts featuring Bob Marley, Snoop Doggy Dog, Johnny Depp, and other faces of the rich and indicted. Their lips move when they read comic books.

Be prepared for disappointment.

I'm very popular, but not every boy wants me. Recently I was invited to this party given by this girl whose sister used to date the drummer for the Red Hot Chili Peppers.

I was wearing a chartreuse micro-mini rubber dress, with my new wing-tip chunky-heel Mary Janes, of course.

And I saw the most gorgeous guy. He looked like Chris O'Donnell with Keanu Reeves's haircut.

So I posed near the onion dip, and suddenly this girl comes out of nowhere and grabs him by the arm.

This is the guy who was supposed to change my life.

I got so depressed.

I went over to the snack table and grabbed this family-size bag of those peanut chocolates, you know, and I went into the bathroom and I ate the whole bag.

I am so weak.

Okay, a word or two about dating. The first rule of dating is:

It's quality not quantity that counts.

I don't want to do massive pages on dating. It's kind of a very personal choice. My suggestion: Watch *Oprah*, *Geraldo*, *Ricki Lake* . . . and if you still want to date after that, go girl.

People ask me lots of questions about dating. Like everyone thinks I'm a major influence in this area, while the real deal is I've pretty much avoided linking the words *boy* and *friend* for most of my life. But I do know that brutal bantering is one of the foremost signs of dating interest.

Bantering, for those who live below Sunset, means arguing, disrespecting, or mouthing off discourteously to another.

Josh and I used to take cheap shots at each other. He'd suggest that I was an airhead for watching *Beavis and Butt-head*. "You know, in some parts of the universe, maybe not in Contempo Casuals," he'd say, "but in some parts, Cher, it's considered cool to know what's going on in the world."

And I'd like flutter my lashes at him and say, "Oh, thank you, Josh. I *so* need lessons from you on how to be cool. Tell me the part about Kenny G. again."

Murray and De are way talented at this. They have a dramatic relationship. Personally, I think they were overly influenced by the Ike and Tina Turner movie. At least once a day, they entertain everyone at school with an intense improv. It's made them way popular. All the kids know them, people take sides, discussion groups form during lunch.

So like I'd have to conclude that an entire genre of dating couples really enjoys this.

Here's a lesson from the experts:

"Oh, no, here he comes." Dionne sighs as Murray approaches in embarrassingly low-slung jeans.

"Woman, why didn't you answer my page?"

De cringes. "I *hate* when you call me 'woman.' "

"Where you been all weekend?" Murray demands as kids begin to gather around. "You jeepin' behind my back?"

Dionne starts digging through her bag. "Jeepin'?" she says in this dangerously controlled voice. "No, but speaking of vehicular excitement . . ." Triumphantly, she pulls a shiny length of braided black hair out of her bag. "Perhaps you can explain how this cheap Kmart hair extension got into your backseat?"

"Eeeyew, what's that?" one of the gathered spectators shrieks.

"Yeah," another one demands, turning to Murray. "Tell her, man. Where'd it come from?"

Murray pulls himself up. "I don't know nothing about that," he says. "That must have come off of you."

Bhaaaap! Someone does a buzzer sound and says, "Wrong! Try again, bro."

Dionne says, "Tscha! I do not wear shiny polyester hair, unlike some people, like, say . . . Shawana."

"Ooooo," says the crowd.

Murray's head starts bobbing like one of those tacky backseat dogs. "Sha-wa-na??" He is outraged. "Man, you should get a job at the Fox Network. You have a real talent for fabrication. Shawana!"

"That's right, Shawana," Dionne insists. "And any time you decide you'd rather be with that anorexic bimbette, instead of a woman who's t.b., true blue, just pull up your saggy Calvins and go."

Warning

This is a delicate art.

Do not try it at home.

Do not try it on a first date.

NAVIGATING

The Food Court

The food court or school cafeteria serves several functions at once. The least of these is nourishment.

It is a social hub. A homework exchange. A mochaccino-less bistro in which to see and be seen.

Here are my special tips for navigating the food court:

Reserving Your Table

You've probably already staked out a permanent place in the cafeteria where you and your crew hang. You've got a cellular. Use it! Phone ahead. Make sure your regular table is available. Let the maître d' know if there'll be an extra joining you.

Ordering Wisely

Before you pick up that plastic-wrapped Caesar salad, be sure to ask whether the croutons are oven-baked or pan-fried. The fat grams in a handful of croutons seriously push the envelope of daily fat intake.

Pan-fried croutons are like tiny breaded time bombs.

NEGOTIATING

Grades

So you got your report card, and now you're toast.

You finally see the connection between the words *grounded* and *ground beef.* Your wheels are history. The Club is on your steering column, and the key is in your daddy's pocket. The door to your room only lets you in.

Grades are a fact of life. But you don't have to settle for second best. Get the quality report card you want by following these simple suggestions:

Never accept a first offer.

Grades are just a jumping-off point to start negotiations.

Set your goals high.
Know your teachers.

Be prepared to say whatever they want to hear.

Here are some examples:

Your phys ed teacher lowballed you.

Shed a few tears and tell her that an undeserving male broke your heart, and though you worship volleyball, you were too distraught to concentrate. Agree with her that all men are pigs.

Have an important meeting of the minds.

Discuss industrial waste with your history teacher. Nod emphatically while she unburdens her heart on the subject. Pledge to start a letter-writing campaign to your congressperson about violations of the Clean Air Act.

If necessary, humiliate yourself.

Grovel. Make promises you know you can't keep.

Cher's Visual Aids to . . . Whatever

I have always cared about making a difference, about making the world a happier, more beautiful place.

I sparked a total romance between two adorable teachers, Mr. Hall and Miss Geist.

My ex-stepbrother, Josh, who was always all serious and flanneled out, credits me with bringing out his lighter side.

My main thrill in life is makeovers. They give me a sense of control in a world of chaos.

*D*ating is kind of a very personal choice. My suggestion: Watch *Oprah, Geraldo, Ricki Lake* . . . and if you still want to date after that, go, girl.

*H*igh school is a vast wasteland when it comes to meeting mature quality guys.

My school is ultracompetitive. Dressing is practically an intramural event. Shopping is the Olympics.

My best friend, Dionne, enjoys wearing tall top hats with her whimsical outfits. "Girlfriend!" I cried. "Have you been shopping with Dr. Seuss?"

To successfully make your presence known in high school, you must have attitude. People tell me my attitude is seriously self-assured but not reekingly so.

It's amazing how totally trivial subjects like phys ed are forced upon you. Is there someone who *doesn't* own her own copy of *Cindy Crawford's Aerobicize* or *Buns of Steel?*

The food court or school cafeteria serves several functions. The least of these is nourishment. It is a social hub. A homework exchange. A mochaccino-less bistro in which to see and be seen.

You've probably already staked out a permanent place in the cafeteria. You've got a cellular. Use it! Phone ahead. Make sure your regular table is available.

$\mathbf{I}$f you are a fashion trendsetter, you are going to have followers. Get used to it. Take it as a compliment. It's flattering. Be gracious.

Makeovers

DOING SOMETHING GOOD FOR HUMANITY

My main thrill in life is makeovers. They give me a sense of control in a world of chaos.

A makeover is taking what someone has and way maximizing it to their best advantage. My basic makeover includes doing new makeup, figuring your colors, replanning your wardrobe, restyling your hair.

Sometimes I like to go deeper and will recommend important fitness videos, reading material, and even pronunciation and vocabulary drills. Improving your vocabulary is like an excellent makeover option. Doing something good for humanity is choice, too.

Why do I bother, you ask? You know that famous expression Teacher, heal thyself? Well, it's true. Whenever I get into molding a needy girl, I find myself on quite a self-improvement spree.

You can't do a total makeover.

I mean, if the makeoveree is 5'3" you're not going to get Cindy Crawford no matter what. Not even the boldest platforms can compensate for a six-inch height differential.

Be realistic in your goals.

You know, like you've spent two weeks cleaning the refrigerator a bite at a time, and you go to your hairdresser with a shot of Kate Moss and say, "This is what I want to look like." It's like, right, your hairdresser can really trim your bangs and forty pounds of excess flesh at the same time.

Always check your motives before you get emotionally involved in a makeover. Here are some you may want to consider:

Right reasons:

Doing something good for humanity.
Taking a lost soul and making her well dressed and popular.
Knowing a life will be better because of you.
Rescuing a potential hottie from a lonely teenage limbo because you know the wounds of adolescence can take years to heal.

Wrong reasons:

Having an urge to dress someone up, but you're too old to play with Barbie dolls. Wanting to check out a rad new look without personally becoming an object of ridicule. Finding someone even more clueless than you are to worship you.

Every girl deserves a
makeover.
It is a second chance
at life.

Making a Contribution

My ex-stepbrother, Josh, is a Baldwin. He's got twinkling blue eyes; thick, dark, curly hair; and a smile that cost Daddy a fortune in braces and maintenance.

Josh is in college. He's majorly into doing stuff for good causes. And lecturing me on my selfishness.

Like when I made fun of the fact that Marky Mark, the poster boy for droopy jeans, was going to plant a tree for Josh's environmental group, Josh went ballistic.

"Maybe Marky Mark wants to use his popularity for a good cause," he growled. "Maybe he wants to make a contribution. In case you've never heard of it, a contribution is the giving of time or funds to assist a needy person or cause."

"Excuse me," I said, "but I have donated many Italian shoes to Lucy, our maid. And when I get my license, I fully intend to brake for animals."

Josh was not impressed. But when I joined Miss Geist's Pismo Beach Disaster Relief Committee at school, everything changed.

Getting involved in good causes at school is a great way to get noticed by Baldwins like Josh! Here are some tips to get you started:

How to recognize guys who are into social change and environmental improvement:

1 ● They wear flannel shirts and read hardcover books, some of which are not even required reading!

2 ● They only go to like three stores at the mall: The Gap, Nature Company, and GNC.

3 ● They can't dance.

Advantages of being a do-gooder:

1 ● College boys are furiously impressed.

2 ● You can get rid of old clothes without guilt. (Please note: Giving attractive, barely worn outfits to beloved members of your domestic staff apparently does not qualify as making a contribution. Collecting them for flood, famine, or hurricane relief victims whom you don't even know does. Duh!)

3 ● Your family can get a tax break.

4 ● It makes you feel great—and look great, too . . . especially if you carry all the stuff you're giving away out to the car by yourself! It's like a total calorie burner.

STRESS MANAGEMENT

Making the Most of the Mall

Sources of stress:

Report cards.

Massive weekend homework assignments.

Getting traffic tickets before you even have your license.

Flat hair.

Signs of stress:

Tow-away zone.

When I find myself in times of trouble, I hit the mall with a red-hot vengeance. Shopping is brutally therapeutic. And going to a mall is like a total rehab. Think of it as a shopping spa. There's nothing that a pocketful of plastic and an acre of purchasing possibilities can't cure.

When a friend is feeling blue, I'll go: "Let's blow off seventh and eighth, and go to the mall. We can walk around, see the new Christian Slater, and gorge calories at CPK."

How do *I* spell relief?
G-a-l-l-e-r-i-a.

For me a mall is a little perfect planet.
It's like being inside a biosphere,
but with air conditioning.

Sometimes hunger can get you all tense. The mall is a great place to load up on stress-cutting carbs. Pasta is especially good. It attacks tension like little gnocchi-shaped piranhas.

But be sensible. Learn how to order responsibly. I mean, the goal here is not to become a heifer. After your waiter introduces himself, just say this:

"Hi, Brad. Angel hair pasta, no oil, no butter, no cheese, with sauce on the side and a green salad, no dressing with balsamic vinegar on the side and Diet Coke with lime but no ice. You've got great hair. Did you color it yourself?"

Never buy anything that says:
Born to Shop
or
When the going gets tough,
the tough go shopping.

Never engage in Buyer's Remorse.

Music

WHY YOU SHOULD BE TOLERANT OF THE ROLLING STONES

Elton Lozoff is way popular. He's like the social director of the Crew. Plus his dad can get you into *any* concert.

Elton is brutally now in his music choices. His Watchman is turned to MTV all day long. He never carries fewer than a dozen CDs with him. He's always shuffling through them during classes. He had this major crisis in debate once when Mr. Hall was talking about political asylum.

Elton's hand shot up. Mr. Hall looked shocked but pleased. "Elton, comments?" he asked.

"I can't find my Smashing Pumpkins," Elton said. "Can I go to the Quad and look before someone snags it?"

Travis is into music, too, and tolerance. Here's an insight he had:

> The way you feel about the Rolling Stones is like the way your kids will feel about Nine Inch Nails, so you shouldn't torment your mother about Mick Jagger anymore.

Music is a family affair for Elton. It's in his blood.

His dad's in the business, and if you even say you think Luscious Jackson is ripe and Elton disagrees, he gets all, "Do you even *know* who my father is?"

Elton's dad gets tickets to everything: Coolio, Counting Crows, Radiohead, The Muffs, Beastie Boys, Lightning Seeds, whatever.

His mom was practically sitting in Streisand's lap in Vegas.

His grandmother is a Deadhead. If she's nice to Elton's dad, you know, like apologizes for ruining his life and all, he gets her into Grateful Dead events all over the country. She once tore a T-shirt off Jerry Garcia.

Partying

YOUR FOREMOST EXTRACURRICULAR EVENT

Avoid parties in the Valley.

The police usually shut them down in less than an hour, and it takes almost that long to get there.

I made the mistake of going to a Val party with Tai when I was trying to fix her up with Elton. Within five minutes of our arrival, she was out cold.

We were dancing, and a girl across the room did this excessively energetic kick. Her clog flew off and hit Tai in the head. Tai crumpled like Kleenex.

We carried her into the kitchen. I told Elton to ask her stuff to make sure she didn't have a concussion. He goes, "Tai, Tai! What's seven times seven?"

Right. "Ask her stuff she knows," I said.

Things you can say to escape a random party:

"My trainer's coming real early."

"Does cooler stain? This is *so* not fixable."

"My grandmother is beeping me. She just
   fell down and she can't get up."

"Who said anything about a time warp?
   I love the twist."

The last time I went to a party in the Valley, I got robbed on the way home.

This teenage psycho in a hooded sweatshirt he probably lifted from Wal-Mart pointed a gun at me and told me to hand over my bag and my beeper, and get down on the ground, facedown.

"But I'm wearing a designer original," I

said. "And what good is my beeper to you? You want my dad paging you?"

He got like really annoyed and started yelling. And he did have a gun. So of course, I got down. It was such a sadistic touch. He grabbed the stuff and ran away. Two whole seconds it took. I totally trashed my dress.

Personal Perfection

FROM AEROBICS TO LIPOSUCTION

I'm not trying to brag or anything,
but my life is so fun, it's like:
Help! I'm trapped in a Noxzema commercial.

*C*all me a perfectionist. I believe in healthful eating, step workouts, French manicures, and always trimming your split ends. I work brutally hard to achieve balance, beauty, and compliments. My friends and I stride through our high school halls, styled hair cleanly bouncing, makeup salon-fresh, fat-free bodies aerobicized to sinewy perfection. We are the world, we are the in crowd.

Basically, we're beautiful, rich, and happy.

If you want to be like us, you've got to do what we do. The good news is, you can! The bad news is, it's better if your dad is really, really rich.

Here are some health and beauty secrets to get started:

Hair tips:

Monday is a universal bad hair day.

Big hair is *not* back.

Complicated hairstyles are *so* over—French braids are practically Jurassic.

Humidity is not your friend.

Makeup:

Makeup is clothing for the skin. You don't wear the same stuff for daytime that you would for major evening social events . . . unless you're the artist formerly known as Prince.

Daddy says he wants to see me apply myself to something besides makeup.

It's easy to endorse the Natural Look if you're Tyra Banks or Christy Turlington, maybe. Or even Michael Jackson . . . Not even!

The right lighting can be as flattering as makeup. Try rosy pink lightbulbs. Use the dimmer switch. Find a warm look that is cosmetically complimentary, but where you don't need a cane to get around.

Managing your weight:

Steak is basically broiled cholesterol. Butter
is to your arteries what fur balls are
to your cat.

Hurling is not a solution.
(Plus it's viciously unattractive.)

I shouldn't even be giving diet advice. I'm
such a heifer, I had two bowls of
Special K today.

Fishing for compliments—
a word of caution.

You ask someone how you look. If they say,
"I'm sorry, I'm very honest. I *have* to say
what I think." You go, "Why?"

Fashion traps to avoid and things that are _so_ last season:

Ripped jeans, tattoos, bell bottoms, white lipstick, spandex, grunge-wear, lip, eye, and cheek rings.

Everything Madonna, especially cone-shaped bustiers.

Everything _Lion King_, except Elton John.

Big hair.

Should you consider cosmetic surgery?

Many famous individuals choose surgical enhancement.

My dad once dated this TV starlet who we called the Bionic Actress. She had like maybe zero left on her entire body that hadn't been surgically improved. She even had liposuction on her ankles.

Some parents do not understand why kids would want to spend a week in the hospital. When our friend Summer told her mother she wanted a nose job for her sixteenth birthday, her mom asked if she'd like malaria for her seventeenth.

Recommended Reading

Personal perfection includes improving your mind, too. Reading is a good way to work on this all-important area. I recommend reading one nonschool book a week. Choose from any of the following for good self-improvement value: *Cindy Crawford's Aerobicize*; *Buns of Steel*; *Fat to Fit*; *Men Are from Mars, Women Are from Venus*.

You might also enjoy *The Bridges of Madison County*. It is a good reminder that grown-ups have feelings, too. It totally reminded me of Mr. Hall and Miss Geist's romance, which De and I worked really hard on. This book is very short and way easy to read, and it shows how adorable old people can be.

Schedules

SNAGGING THE CLASSES THAT WORK FOR YOU

School is important, but face it, it's not all *that*. Your time is valuable. So you want to schedule your classes to allow for personal growth in *all* areas—except your hips, of course. You'll want to save time for such extracurricular activities as driver's ed, aerobics, shopping, pedicures, and other important transformational experiences.

Here are some things to consider when working out that excellent school schedule:

● **Health Needs:** What time can your personal trainer fit you in? (Fabianne, my masseuse, says I hold a lot of tension.)

● **Daytime TV:** Are there any major trials being televised? Is there a truly startling guest on *Oprah?*

● **Current Events:** Will you miss the debut of a brutally hot new video on MTV?

● Never settle for a class schedule that makes you miss the soaps.

● Classes to try to get: debate. Debate teaches an essential adolescent skill: arguing to win.

I mean, what's the use of accepting comments like "You're grounded" and "You call these grades?" when there is an actual class that shows you how to ward off your parents' bitterness and threats.

I got so much out of debate. Like I did this oral on "Violence in the Media."

Basically, I said how the attorney general says there's too much violence on TV and that it should stop . . . because people will watch violent TV and want to try it.

So I said, even if you took off all the violent shows, people could still see violence on the news, so there's no point taking it out of shows that need it for entertainment value.

I pulled an excellent response to my speech. Except, of course, from Amber, who is renowned for her negativity.

"Hello, excuse me," Amber goes. "Was I the only one listening? I mean, I thought it reeked."

"I think," I said, "that's your designer imposter perfume."

That's what you learn in debate.

Tardies

YOUR TWO BASIC APPROACHES

If you even have a life, you're bound to be late to class sometimes. This is called being tardy. Tardies go on your record and can influence your grades. So I personally believe in arguing rampantly against them. But there are two basic approaches to tardies: denial and acceptance. Here are examples:

Denial

When Mr. Hall, my debate teacher, announced that I had two tardies, I raised my hand, stood up, and said, "I object."

Mr. Hall closed his eyes as if in prayer. "Cher, does everything have to be a negotiation with you?"

"Do you recall the dates of the alleged tardies?" I asked.

"One was last Monday."

"Mr. Hall, did you taste the vegetarian chili in the Quad on Monday?" I demanded. "Half the school was hurling in the lounges. I was deadly ill."

I know how Mr. Hall hates the food in the Quad. "All right," he said. "I'll let one of them slide."

Tscha!

Acceptance

Travis Birkenstock, everyone's favorite long-haired space traveler, handled it differently.

"Congratulations," Mr. Hall said to him. "By far the most tardies in the class. Thirty-eight in all. A near-perfect record."

The class did an Arsenio—waving and whooping as Travis, skateboard tucked under his arm, stood up to take a bow. His hair flopped forward.

"Thank you, thank you." He was all grinning gladness. "This is so unexpected. I didn't even have a speech prepared. . . . But I would like to say this . . . tardiness is not something you can do all on your own. Many, many people had to contribute. I'd like to thank my parents for never driving me to school. And the L.A. bus drivers for taking a chance on an unknown kid. And last but not least, the wonderful crew at McDonald's, for the long hours they spend making Egg McMuffins, without which I might never be tardy. Thank you."

Wheels

WHINING AND WHEEDLING FOR THE CAR OF YOUR DREAMS

Preparing Your Parents

It's easier than you think to get wheels. After all, you have to have something to practice for your road test in. And your parents aren't really going to let you tear up the Jag, right?

It's a little harder to get the kind of loqued-out machine that'll win you major peer status points. Try making up excellent economic and safety statistics on the car of your dreams. Then tell your dad you're quoting *Consumer Reports* or *Car and Driver*.

Parking

Some people think it's really important to learn how to park. But what's the point? Everywhere you go there's valet.

Road tests and other obstacles

Look at the lines painted on the road. Pick a pair and stay inside them.

Two permits do not equal a license.

Never wear platform shoes to your road test.

A red octagon is a Stop sign.

If you pass one, police do not usually accept the explanation "I totally paused."

Why I failed my first road test:

The DMV tester said, "Move into the right lane." So I did.

Then he screamed, "Watch out for the BIKE RIDER!" So I swerved back into my lane and this wild-eyed person on a bicycle whizzed by perfectly unharmed.

After that I stayed in the middle of the road.

But the tester said, "You're taking up both lanes. Police frown on that, you know. Get in the right lane."

"But I'm afraid I'll scrape the parked cars," I told him.

"You can't have the whole road to yourself," he said.

So I went to my right, and of course I scraped a parked car.

So then the tester starts yelling, "NOT SO CLOSE!"

"Should I leave them a note?" I asked.

"Pull over and turn off the engine," he said.

"Is that it? Did I pass?"

"Hmmm, let's see." He checked his notes. "You can't park, switch lanes, make right-hand turns, make left-hand turns, you've damaged private property, and almost killed someone. Offhand, I'd say . . . you failed."

A Word to the Clueless

You are not alone.
Think of all the people on *Baywatch*.

About the Author

H. B. Gilmour is the author of the bestselling novelizations *Clueless* and *Pretty in Pink,* as well as *Clueless™: Achieving Personal Perfection; Clarissa Explains It All: Boys;* the well-reviewed young-adult novel *Ask Me If I Care;* and more than fifteen other books for adults and young people.

Boys. Clothes. Popularity. Whatever!

Based on the major motion picture from Paramount
A novel by H.B. Gilmour
○ 53631-1/$4.99

Cher Negotiates New York
by Jennifer Baker ○ 56868-X/$4.99

An American Betty in Paris
by Randi Reisfeld ○ 56869-8/$4.99

Achieving Personal Perfection
by H.B. Gilmour ○ 56870-1/$4.99

Cher's Guide to ... Whatever
by H.B. Gilmour ○ 56865-5/$4.99

And Based on the ABC-TV Prime Time Series

Cher Goes Enviro-Mental
by Randi Reisfeld ○ 00324-0/$3.99